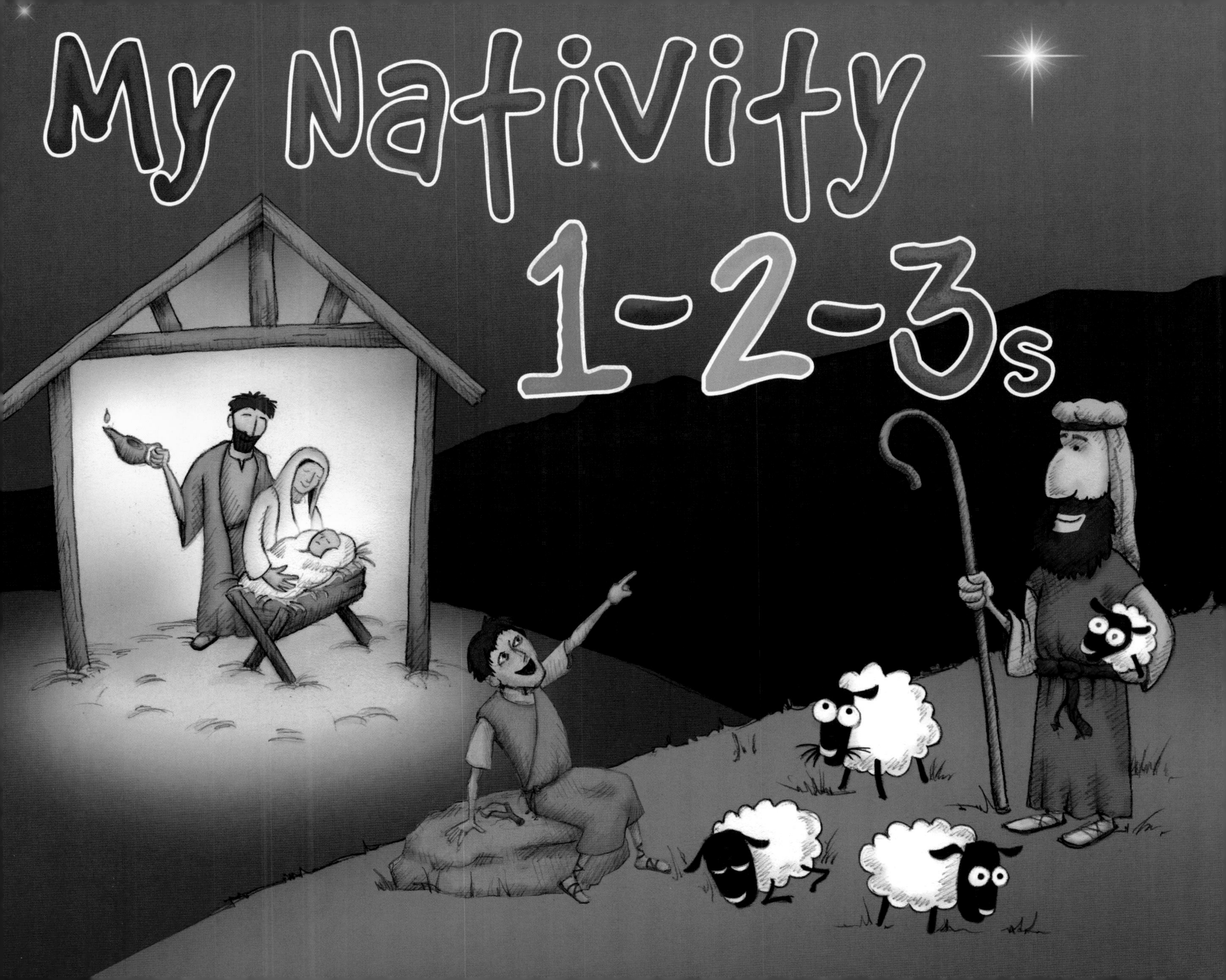
My Nativity
1-2-3s

For Taisei, Mirei, Leina, Adele, Samuel, Ezra, Malachi, Elysee, Jane, and "my" Primary children in Lindon 10th.
— Esther

Text © 2018 Esther Yu Sumner
Illustrations © 2018 Robert Davis
All rights reserved.

The opinions and views expressed herein belong solely to the author and do not necessarily represent the opinions or views of Cedar Fort, Inc. Permission for the use of sources, graphics, and photos is also solely the responsibility of the author.

ISBN 13: 978-1-4621-2246-2

Published by Plain Sight Publishing, an imprint of Cedar Fort, Inc.
2373 W. 700 S., Springville, UT 84663
Distributed by Cedar Fort, Inc., www.cedarfort.com

Library of Congress Control Number: 2018946713

Cover design and interior layout design by Shawnda T. Craig
Cover design © 2018 Cedar Fort, Inc.
Edited by Kaitlin Barwick

Printed in the United States of America

10 9 8 7 6 5 4 3 2 1

Printed on acid-free paper

My Nativity 1-2-3s

written by **Esther Yu Sumner**

Illustrated by **Robert Davis**

Plain Sight Publishing • An imprint of Cedar Fort, Inc. • Springville, Utah

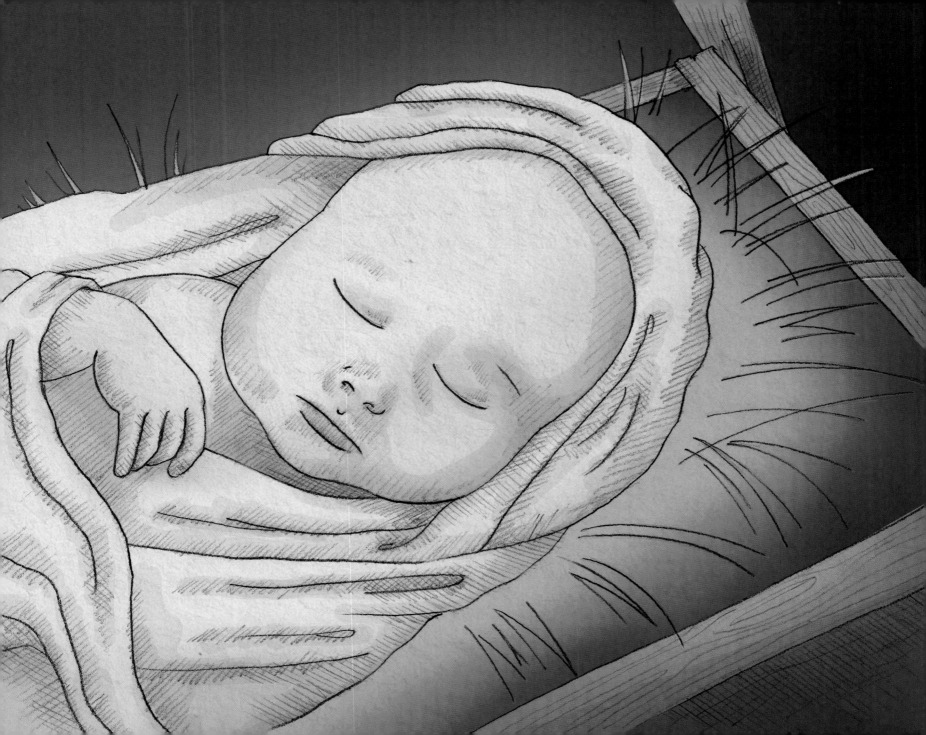

3 gifts

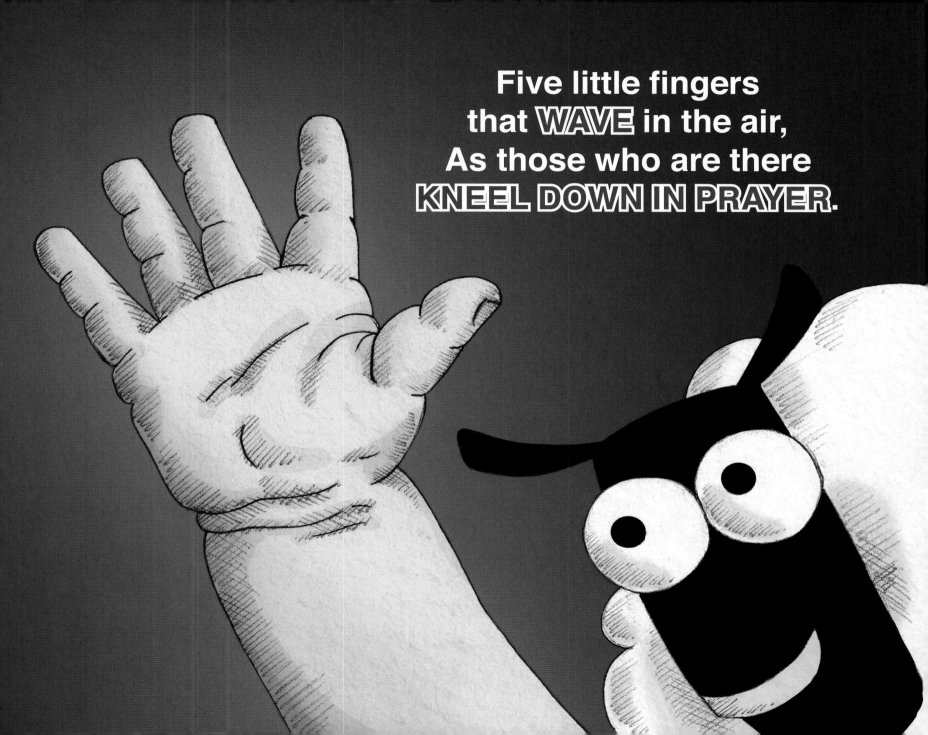

Six names were used by
the **ANGEL** who came,
To **HONOR** the one
who'd heal the lame.

6
names

Seven sheep LOOK UP at the hosts in the sky, where angels burst forth in SONGS FROM ON HIGH.

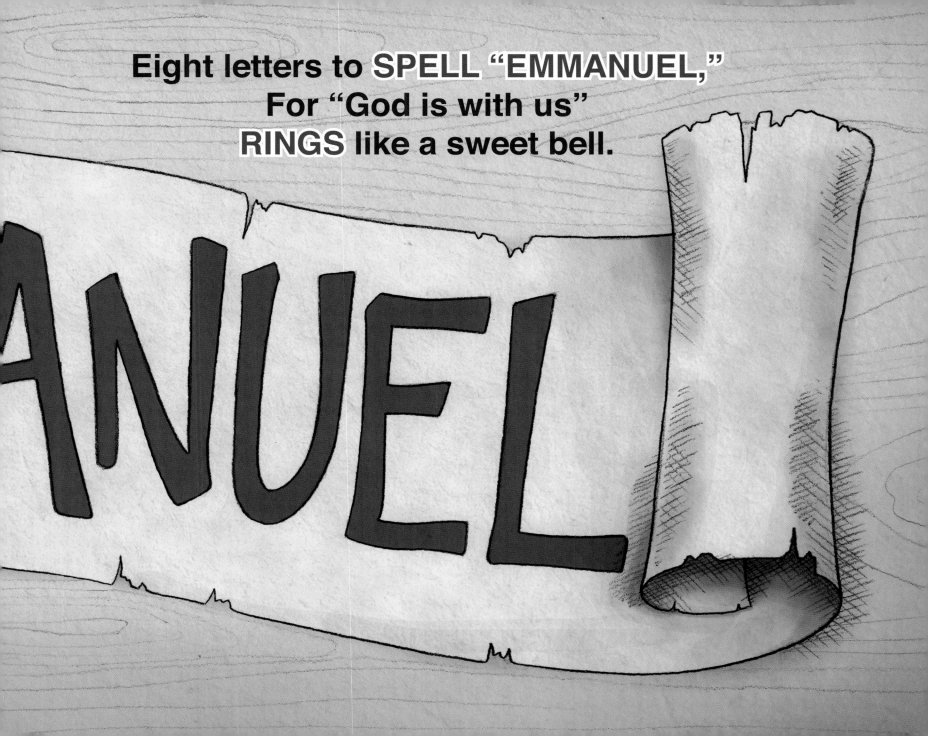

Eight letters to SPELL "EMMANUEL,"
For "God is with us"
RINGS like a sweet bell.

9 symbols

Nine symbols REMIND US
of when He was sent,
They help us REMEMBER
this special event.

Ten little toes and
two little eyes,
REMIND US HE'S LIKE US,
this one that's so wise.

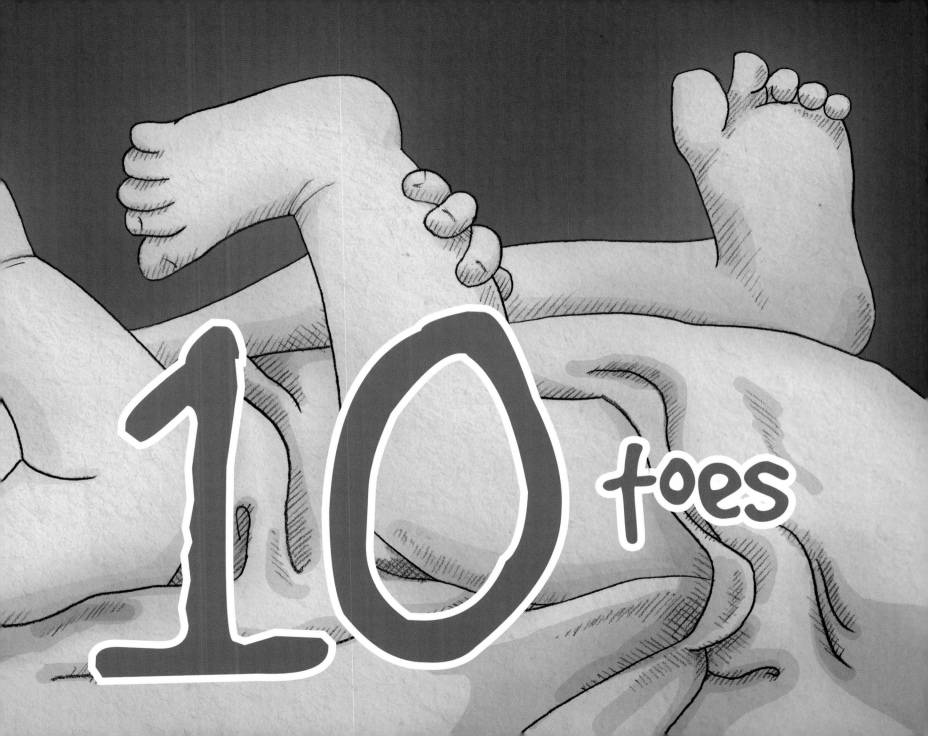

11 camels

Eleven camels **FILLED** with good cheer,
For each one knows their **KING IS NEAR**.

Twelve trees **BEND** for the carpenter's son,
For even they know that **HE'S THE ONE**.

1 baby

2 new parents

3 gifts

4 shepherds

5 fingers

6 names

10 toes

11 camels

12 trees

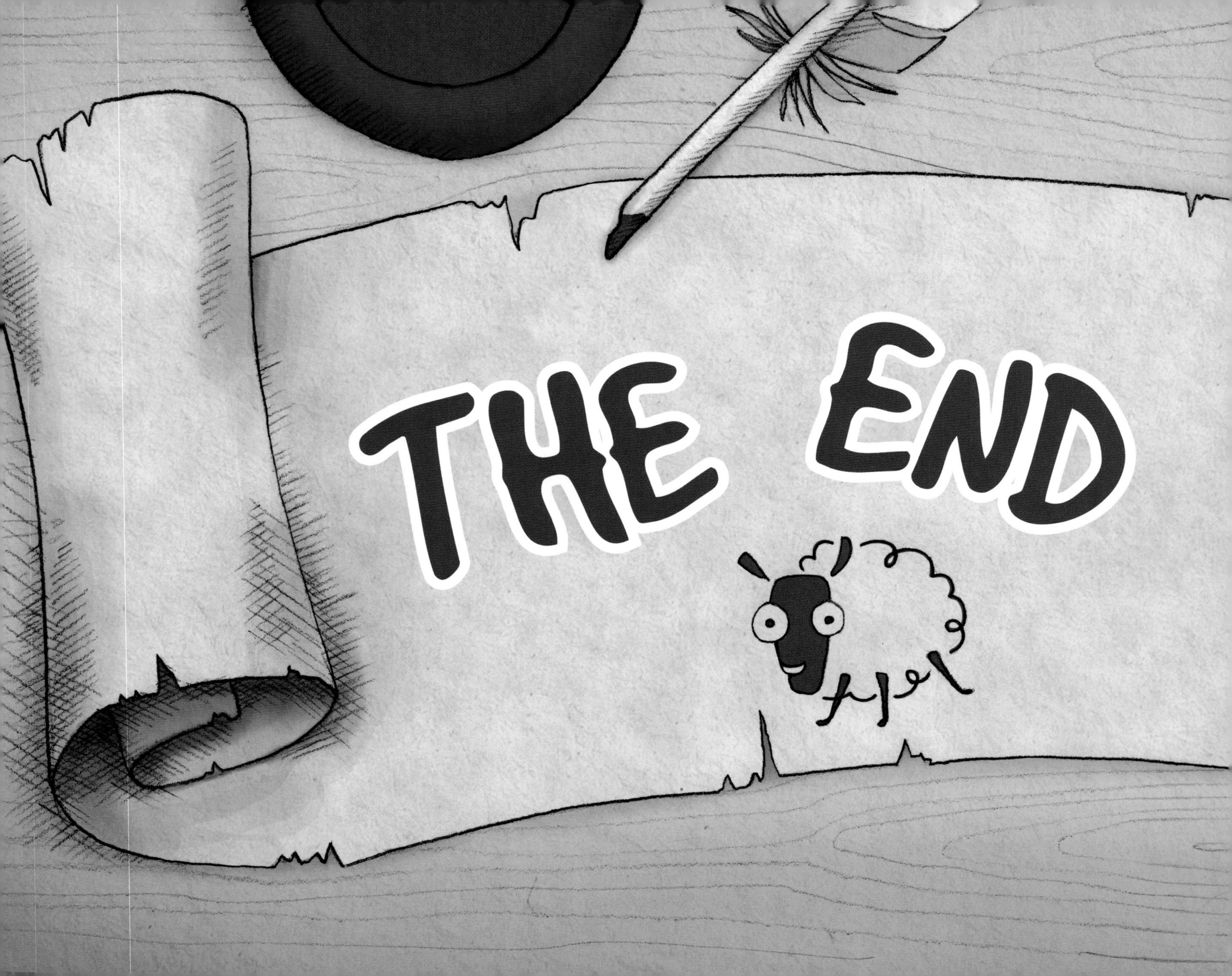
THE END